WILD WEST WOMEN

KATHERINE KROHN

In Consultation with Martha Cosgrove,
M.A. and Reading Specialist

JUST THE FACTS BIOGRAPHIES

LERNER PUBLICATIONS COMPANY/MINNEAPOLIS

For my mother, Betty Stevens Krohn

Martha Cosgrove has a master's degree from the University of Minnesota in secondary education, with an emphasis on developmental and remedial reading. She is licensed in 7–12 English and language arts, developmental reading, and remedial reading. She has had several works published, and she gives numerous state and national presentations in her areas of expertise.

Lerner Publications Company
A division of Lerner Publishing Group, Inc.
241 First Avenue North
Minneapolis, MN 55401 U.S.A.

Website address: www.lernerbooks.com

Library of Congress-in-Publication Data

Krohn, Katherine E.
    Wild West women / by Katherine Krohn.
        p.   cm. – (Just the facts biographies)
    Includes bibliographical references and index.
    ISBN-13: 978–0–8225–2646–9 (lib. bdg. : alk. paper)
    ISBN-10: 0–8225–2646–8 (lib. bdg. : alk. paper)
    1. Women pioneers—West (U.S.)—Biography—Juvenile literature. 2. West (U.S.)—Biography—Juvenile literature. 3. Frontier and pioneer life—West (U.S.)—Juvenile literature. I. Title. II. Series.
F596.K75 2006
978–dc22   2005013567

Manufactured in the United States of America
3 – CG – 7/1/13

CONTENTS

CHAPTER 1

ADVENTURE AND HARDSHIP

(Above) Calamity Jane became a legend in her own time.

ONE DAY IN THE 1870S, Martha Jane Cannary walked toward the bar in a saloon in Deadwood, in modern-day South Dakota. Better known as Calamity Jane, Martha was tall and tough. She believed that she was as strong as any man. She also liked to have as much fun as any man. Calamity held her gun and fired a bullet into the ceiling of the tavern. The men shouted and laughed. The bartender chuckled and gave her a drink.

The women of Deadwood, where Calamity lived, were shocked by her "unfeminine" behavior. But most of the men in town thought of her as a celebrity. One pioneer remembered meeting Calamity: "I said, 'Who is that loud-mouthed man' and [somebody] said, 'That ain't no man, that's Calamity Jane!' "

Of course, not all the women who settled in the American West in the 1800s were as colorful and famous as Calamity Jane. Still, Calamity stands as a symbol of the free and independent spirit inside every pioneering woman.

FIRST STEPS

During the late 1800s, women of all ages, backgrounds, and races settled in the western United States, an area called the Wild West. Most of these adventurous women led quieter lives than the famous Calamity Jane.

Long before the pioneers moved west in the 1800s, women and men were already living on the land. In fact, Native Americans were living on the land that became the United States for hundreds of years before Europeans arrived. The Native Americans formed more than three hundred tribes.

Native Americans lived in North and South America long before Europeans arrived in the late 1400s. About 40,000 Indians lived at this settlement located in modern-day Illinois.

They spread across North and South America. Each tribe followed its own traditions and spoke its own language. Some of the tribes farmed. Others hunted for food and furs. Some of the people built homes from animal hides. Others made large villages out of earth.

In the late 1400s, European explorers began to visit North and South America, which they called the New World. They came in search of riches. They liked what they found in the New World—gold, silver, furs, and land. For the next four hundred years, a steady stream of European settlers came to the New World. They took over much of the Native Americans' land. Many tribes lost their homes, their culture, and often even their lives.

IT'S A FACT!

In the late 1400s, when Europeans first came to North America, millions of Native Americans were living on the land. By 1900, this population figure had dropped to only about 250,000. Wars and disease caused the severe drop.

THE GREAT FRONTIER

In 1776, the United States of America became a new nation. The new U.S. government decided that the border between Native American lands and U.S. territory would be the Appalachian Mountains. These peaks rise near the eastern coast of the United States. But this border didn't last long. Through treaties (agreements) and war, the

U.S. government forced the Native Americans to move farther and farther west.

In 1803, the United States bought the large Louisiana Territory from France. The territory was 828,000 square miles of land between the Mississippi River and the Rocky Mountains. The Louisiana Purchase doubled the size of the United States. The next year, President Thomas Jefferson asked Captain Meriwether Lewis and William Clark to explore the territory. President Jefferson hoped that Lewis and Clark would help

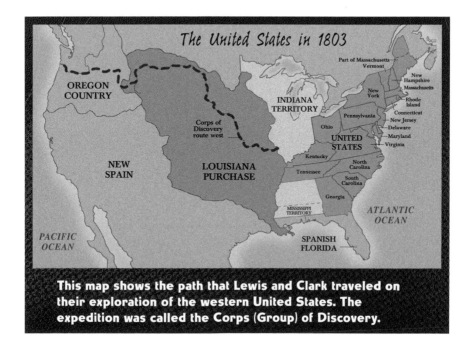

This map shows the path that Lewis and Clark traveled on their exploration of the western United States. The expedition was called the Corps (Group) of Discovery.

fur traders connect with Native American tribes in the West. He also hoped the explorers would find a water passage from the Mississippi River westward to the Pacific Ocean. Americans had long dreamed of such a route, which they called the Northwest Passage.

Many Native Americans were helpful in guiding Lewis and Clark through the territory. In present-day North Dakota, Mandan and Minitari Indians gave the explorers information about the path of the Missouri River. Later in the journey, a Shoshone woman, Sacagawea, joined the expedition as a guide. She spoke English as well as other Native American languages. She helped Lewis and Clark understand what the Indians they met were saying.

Although Lewis and Clark did not find a Northwest Passage, they learned a lot about the western land and its peoples. They also became the first white men to cross the western half of the United States. Their expedition made it possible for people of the eastern United States to move west of the Mississippi River. At this time, the land west of the river was mostly unclaimed by white men and women.

SACAGAWEA

Sacagawea, born around 1788 in Idaho, was a member of the Shoshone Indian tribe. When she was about ten years old, she was kidnapped and sold to a French Canadian trader, Toussaint Charbonneau, who made her his wife.

When explorers Lewis and Clark were traveling along the Missouri River, they met Charbonneau and made a deal with him. Both he and his wife would join the group. Sacagawea helped the group talk to the Native people they met.

Some historians believe that the young woman may have been forced to help. Whatever the case, Sacagawea had no way of knowing that the Lewis and Clark expedition would eventually lead to settlers taking over Native American lands.

Sacagawea was part of the Shoshone tribe.

This type of wagon was called a Conestoga. It was named after the town of Conestoga, Pennsylvania, where the wagon was made.

WESTWARD MOVEMENT

In 1837, the United States faced an economic depression. Banks closed, and many people lost their jobs. At the same time, people heard tales of a western "paradise." People talked about free, rich farmland and forests thick with timber and animals to hunt. Many people couldn't resist the stories. They packed their bags and headed westward.

While settlers built new lives for themselves, Native Americans suffered. In the 1830s, President Andrew Jackson signed the Indian Removal Act. The law gave the U.S. government the power to force Native Americans to move to lands west of the Mississippi River.

SARAH WINNEMUCCA

When Sarah Winnemucca was born in 1844, her parents gave her the name Thocmetony, which means "shell flower." Thocmetony was a Paiute Indian. Her grandfather was an important tribal leader, Chief Truckee.

The Paiute people were hunters who killed game and gathered wild food in the deserts of northwestern Nevada, northeastern California, and southeastern Oregon. They were known as a peaceful people.

By the mid-1800s, many northern Indian tribes in the United States were being forced off their land by white settlers. Chief Truckee believed that the Paiute and other tribes could live peacefully with white people. Truckee served as a guide to many travelers and had many white friends.

Sarah Winnemucca

Chief Truckee thought it was wise to learn the ways of the white people. In 1850, he took his family on a trip to California. Wherever they traveled, people greeted them with friendliness. Thocmetony's grandfather was well liked by the settlers. They even gave six-year-old Thocmetony a white name. They called her Sarah.

In 1857, Chief Truckee arranged for his granddaughters, Sarah and Elma, to live with a white family. A friend of his, Major Ormsby, ran a store with his wife in what would become Genoa, Nevada. The girls would work in the Ormsby's store. They would help with chores and care for the couple's nine-year-old daughter.

Sarah and her sister became part of the Ormsby family. They got rid of their Native clothing and wore long dresses. Mrs. Ormsby taught the girls how to read and write. Sarah and her sister quickly adjusted to this very different life. Within a year, Sarah could speak English very well.

As more and more white Americans moved west, the Paiutes, like other Indian nations, were pushed westward. Finally, they were forced to live on a reservation (an area of land set aside for Native Americans) in Washington. Sarah watched helplessly as the U.S. government broke promises and lied to the Paiutes, causing many of them to starve.

In 1883, Sarah toured the country, giving public lectures. She spoke for the Paiute people. But her speeches made little difference. Sarah felt like a failure for not being able to help her people more. But that year, she became the first Native American woman to publish a book in the United States. The book, *Life among the Paiutes,* told about her tribe's culture and beliefs. She died on October 17, 1891. Her work inspired later Paiute Indians to work for their rights and to hold on to their tribal traditions.

The United States continued to expand its territory during the 1840s and 1850s. In 1845, Texas became the twenty-eighth state. A year later, the United States gained Oregon Country in the Northwest. In 1848, after a two-year war, Mexico gave up the entire Southwest, from Texas to California, to the U.S. government.

In 1848, a mill worker in California discovered gold. Within a year, more than eighty thousand people headed westward, hoping to strike it rich. Boomtowns (towns that quickly sprang up around

More than eighty thousand people went west to California after gold was discovered there in 1848.

mining areas) filled with people. At first, most of these people were men. But as mining areas in California, Oregon, and South Dakota grew, women went there too. Some joined their husbands. Others looked for gold, land, husbands, or jobs.

Some women made money by running businesses. Mary Jane Caples, a miner's wife, started a baking business. "I [decided] to make some pies and see if I could sell them to the miners for their lunches," she said. "I sold fruit pies for one dollar and a quarter a piece, and mince pies

This woman set up a business in California doing laundry and mending.

for one dollar and fifty cents. I sometimes made and sold a hundred in a day"

Another miner's wife, Luzena Stanley Wilson, wanted to run a restaurant during the California gold rush. But she didn't have a building. Wilson bought some boards and built a table outdoors, under the trees. "I bought [food] at a neighboring store, and when my husband came back at night he found, [under] the weird light of the pine torches, twenty miners eating at my table," she recalled. "Each man as he rose

put a dollar in my hand and said I might count him as a permanent customer."

Although the gold rush brought riches to some, many miners didn't find a thing. But people soon had another reason to go west. In 1862, President Abraham Lincoln signed the Homestead Act. This allowed any U.S. citizen to claim 160 acres of free land. In return, the settlers–called homesteaders–had to work the land and remain there for at least five years.

Between 1840 and 1870, more than three hundred thousand people traveled westward on the overland trails. Some major routes included the Oregon Trail, the California Trail, the Santa Fe Trail, and the Mormon Trail. Most of the pioneers were men, but thousands of women came too. All the travelers

IT'S A FACT!

Women took advantage of the Homestead Act too. One woman named Anetta Daisy claimed land four different times. She was shot twice, both times by people who wanted the same piece of land she was claiming. Neither bullet kept her from keeping her four plots of land.

were searching for better opportunities. Along the way, they saw new lands. They battled diseases, severe weather, and other dangers.

The newcomers also met the native peoples of the land. Many Native Americans found the settlers strange and disrespectful. The white people thought they owned the land, the air, and the water.

THE TRAIL OF TEARS

In the winter of 1838, the U.S. Army marched almost all the members of the Cherokee Nation from their homeland in Georgia westward to Oklahoma. The journey was long and hard. Food was scarce. About four thousand Cherokee died along the way. This forced journey later became known as the Trail of Tears.

Cherokee Indians travel west on the Trail of Tears in 1838.

By 1875, the U.S. government had forced most Native American families to move to reservations (areas of land set aside for them). Many Native Americans were killed as they tried to defend their families and homes. At the same time, the flood of white people moving westward continued. Between 1877 and 1887, 4.5 million more people came to the West.

By 1890, no more land was available for homesteaders to claim. But for almost twenty more years, the spirit of the West remained wild and changing.

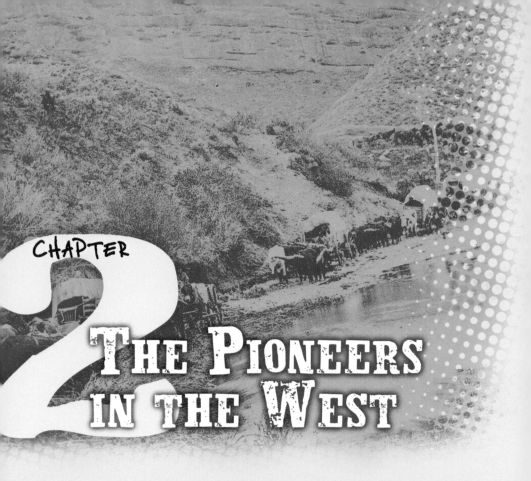

2 THE PIONEERS IN THE WEST

(Above) A wagon train makes its way through thick mud in Utah.

MANY OF THE WOMEN of the early American West wrote about their lives in diaries, travel journals, letters, newspaper articles, and stories. For some women, the life was an exciting adventure. For others, traveling and making a home in the West was full of hardship and heartache.

OVERLAND TALES

Eliza Hustler, born in Illinois, made the trip west
to Oregon in 1847 when she was thirteen. Her
family arrived in Oregon without any problems,
although a baby girl in their wagon train died
during their trip. Later in life, Eliza recalled her
childhood journey. "I can still see the plains with
the shimmering heat waves, the dark masses of
buffalo moving over the rolling hills. . . . " For other
women, the overland trip was harder. Families
couldn't afford to wear out their animal teams, so
anyone who wasn't driving the wagon usually
had to walk.

A woman's role on the trail was clear. The
women were responsible
for cooking, sewing,
cleaning, and caring for
their children. Women
were also expected to
nurse the sick. They used
natural remedies such as
poke root and willow bark
to bring down a fever.
Sulfur and molasses were
common treatments for

IT'S A FACT!

Many babies died
before the age of one
in the West. Doctors
were scarce. It wasn't
uncommon for
mothers to give birth
to their children
without another
woman to help.

Rest stops for the wagon trains did not mean rest for the women. They still had to cook, clean, and mend clothing for the family.

stomachache. Women on the trail used bread mold on wounds and cuts to fight infection.

Before trail travelers even left home, they were told to take certain supplies with them. Books such as *The Emigrant's Guide to Oregon and California* gave travelers a helpful list of food items to bring. These items included 20 pounds of sugar, 200 pounds of flour, 150 pounds of bacon, 10

pounds of coffee, 10 pounds of salt, plus baking soda, vinegar, tea, and dried beans and peas. Dried fruit was also recommended. It stopped people from getting scurvy. This disease comes from a lack of vitamin C, which can be found in certain fruits. The trip west wasn't cheap. A sturdy wagon, food, medicine, and other supplies cost between $500 and $1,000. (In modern dollars, this is between $10,000 and $20,000.)

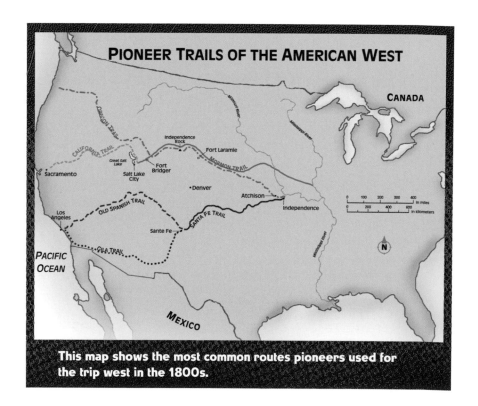

This map shows the most common routes pioneers used for the trip west in the 1800s.

Some overland travelers were lucky enough to have chickens and cows with them on the journey. But most people had to hunt for meat. Many western travelers killed buffalo for food.

Narcissa Whitman, a Christian missionary (religious teacher), liked buffalo meat at first. But when the food she had brought with her on the trip ran out and she had nothing to eat but buffalo, she grew very tired of it. Whitman also ate horse meat on the trail. "I do not prefer it, but can eat it very well when we have nothing else," she said.

MARCUS AND NARCISSA WHITMAN

In 1836, Christian missionaries Marcus and Narcissa Whitman were among the first white people to travel the entire Oregon Trail. The Whitmans started a church among the Cayuse Indians in present-day Washington State.

In 1843, Marcus Whitman returned to the eastern United States and guided the first large party of settlers to Oregon. The wagon train brought deadly diseases, such as measles, to the Cayuse population. Since the diseases couldn't be treated at the time, many of the Cayuse people died. The survivors were angry. They blamed Whitman for the deaths. They also didn't like how the missionaries tried to make them give up their cultural traditions. In November 1847, the Cayuse killed Marcus and Narcissa Whitman and twelve other white settlers.

When people died on the trip west, the travelers had to bury them and move on.

Travelers had to adapt to the different regions they passed through. But no matter how strong they were, the travelers met some problems for which they just weren't prepared. Diseases such as scarlet fever, typhus, and measles could be deadly. At the time, none of these diseases could be cured.

A young Oregon Trail traveler, Abigail Hathaway King, remembered when the fatal illness of cholera struck her wagon train. Her six-month-old brother, Hile, died first, near the Cascade Mountains in Washington. A woman in the wagon

train died later. Abigail's mother helped bury her. Soon Abigail's mother also got the disease.

Abigail remembered, "Father didn't know what to do, so he had her drink a cupful of spirits of camphor. The other people thought it would kill her or cure her. It cured her."

VIRGINIA REED

James Reed had heard about many opportunities in the West. He was excited about moving there and wanted to make the journey as easy as possible for his wife and their four children, Virginia, James, Martha Jane (nicknamed Patty), and Tommy. As the owner of a successful furniture factory, Reed could afford many comforts for his family. He bought a fancy covered wagon for the trip. A small stove kept the wagon's cabin warm. Extra storage space held clothes, medicine, food, and dishes. Two passenger seats built with springs would make the bumpy ride west more comfortable.

Virginia Reed was thirteen years old in April 1846, when her family began its two-thousand-mile overland trip west. From their home in Springfield, Illinois, the Reed family was going to travel along the Oregon Trail, through Wyoming to the

Like thousands of Americans, James and Margaret Reed were drawn westward by the promise of a better life.

California Trail. They had packed their covered wagon with as much as it could carry. But still, they had to leave most of their things—and their comfortable home—in Illinois.

"At last we were all in the wagons, the drivers cracked their whips, the oxen moved slowly forward and the long journey had begun," Virginia remembered. She liked her family's wagon, which she called the Pioneer Palace Car. The wagon had an entrance on the side. This side door opened into a cozy space, almost like a small living room.

In July, the wagon train reached Fort Laramie, Wyoming. There, other wagons joined the group for the journey through the Rocky Mountains. Virginia's father joined a group that was taking a route called Hastings Cutoff. This group, or party, elected George Donner as their leader.

The Donner Party soon learned that the Hastings Cutoff wasn't what they'd hoped it would be. There was no trail to follow. To move forward, they had to hack through thick desert plants. James Reed was worried. His oxen were dying of thirst. Some other drivers planned to search for water for their animals. They agreed to take the Reeds' oxen. But the oxen escaped. The Reeds were stranded in the desert. The family no longer had animals to pull their wagon. Other members of the party took pity on the Reeds and gave them four oxen. But the small team wasn't strong enough to pull the heavy "palace" wagon. The Reeds were forced to leave their big wagon behind and ride in a much smaller wagon.

The Reeds' luck didn't improve. The trip became more difficult and uncertain. People in the party grew angry with one another. In October, Virginia's father had an argument with a man named John Snyder. The men started fighting. In

self-defense, Reed stabbed Snyder to death.

The Donner Party held a meeting that night to decide how to deal with the killing. The people had respected Reed very much before the stabbing. His crime had been in self-defense, so the group decided not to punish him by death. Instead, they forced him to leave the wagon train. They told him to go ahead by himself toward Sutter's Fort, a place where he could find help and supplies. Reed's wife and children stayed behind with the Donner Party.

With only a horse and a little food, James Reed set out across the desert. In the darkness, he saw something moving toward him. At first, he thought it was an animal. But it was his daughter Virginia, who had sneaked away from the wagon party. She handed her father a rifle and ammunition, hugged him, and hurried back to the others.

IT'S A FACT!

James Reed had to cross the snow-covered Sierra Nevada mountains in eastern California to find help. He arrived at Sutter's Fort, which is located in the city that became Sacramento, California. Run by John Sutter, the fort was a place to buy goods.

The Donner Party set up camp. They hoped to survive the long winter in the Sierra Nevada mountains.

It was December, and snow was falling steadily. The Donner Party was forced to camp on the chilly slopes of the mountains, where they found an old log cabin. Virginia, her mother, and a few others crowded in for the long winter. Other families split into groups, built log shelters, and camped nearby.

The members of the Donner Party did their best to stay alive. They had to kill their oxen for food. When the meat was gone, Virginia's mother and the others made soup from the bones that had been thrown away. As time passed, the food supply ran out. Margaret Reed set off with Virginia into the mountains in search of food. But the freezing cold drove them back to the cabin.

Margaret cut strips of rawhide off the roof of their log shelter and boiled the tough hide into a paste. It tasted terrible, but it kept them alive. She also caught field mice, and she even killed her pet dog for food. The Donner Party was desperate. They were starving—three people had died already. Some members of the party made a difficult decision. To keep themselves alive, they ate the flesh of those who had died.

Finally, on February 19, 1847, a rescue party

IT'S A FACT!

Patty Reed, Virginia's little sister, also survived. She held on to a tiny doll throughout her hard time. She brought it with her to Sutter's Fort and kept it all her life. After her death in 1923, this doll became part of an exhibit about Sutter's Fort.

IT'S A FACT!

When Virginia grew up, she became a well-known horse rider. She married John Murphy, one of the first real estate developers in California. When her husband died in 1892, Virginia Reed Murphy took over the business. She became one of the first female real estate agents in California. Virginia died in 1920, at the age of eighty-seven.

from Sutter's Fort arrived, led by Virginia's father. "I can not describe the death-like look they all had," he wrote later in his diary. "Bread Bread Bread was the begging of every child and grown person except my wife."

The rescue party helped the Donner Party cross the difficult mountain passage. A month later, Virginia and her family arrived in California. Of the eighty-seven people in the party, forty-one died.

SETTLING IN

At first, the West seemed full of promise to many new settlers. But in reality, surviving the wilderness was a struggle. Farming the land was hard work. For women, endless chores and the strain of giving birth made many of them look and feel old before they were forty.

A woman stands in the doorway of her home in South Dakota. Life on the frontier was often lonely.

Frontier women were often lonely. Many families were alone in the wilderness, with no neighbors for miles around. A pioneer on the Rogue River in Oregon kept a journal to ease her loneliness and collect her thoughts. "Alone all day [to] finish a new dress," she wrote. "Wish I had some new book to read to pass [the] time. . . . O! dear, I am tired of the same dull monotony of time. . . . [I] think if I had the company of some lively female acquaintance I would feel better."

The women who settled in towns were less lonely, but they often wished for excitement. One early pioneer, born near Salem, Oregon, reported, "Because there were fewer things going on, everybody turned out to public affairs, like hangings, or anything of that kind."

LAURA INGALLS WILDER

Laura Elizabeth Ingalls was born in a log cabin in the "Big Woods" of Pepin, Wisconsin, on February 7, 1867. Laura's "Pa," Charles Ingalls, was a farmer, hunter, and carpenter. Caroline Quiner Ingalls, Laura's mother, valued education and made sure that her children could read from an early age. When Laura was born, she had a two-year-old sister, Mary.

Calling himself a pioneer man, Pa often followed his urges to move. Laura spent her childhood moving from place to place with her family. When she was a baby, her family left Wisconsin and moved southwest to Missouri. But the family didn't stay for long. In 1869, Ingalls moved his family to the prairies (grasslands) of present-day Kansas.

But they didn't stay there long either. In the fall of 1870, the Ingalls family was forced to leave.

Laura *(right)* and her sisters, Carrie *(left)* and Mary *(middle)* lived a frontier life.

The U.S. government had given the land on which they had built a home to the Osage Indians. The family moved back to Wisconsin. There, Laura and Mary went to school in a one-room building called the Barry Corner School.

Still, Pa wasn't happy. In 1874, he bought a piece of land near Walnut Grove, Minnesota. There, Pa figured, he could clear the wooded area and plow fields for farming. The surrounding area was full of wildlife to hunt. The Ingalls family lived in a sod dugout in a creek bank until Pa could

build a wooden house. Dugouts were homes made by digging into a bank of earth. The roof of a sod house was made of sections or strips cut from the grass-covered ground.

Laura and her sisters attended school in nearby Walnut Grove. Laura's favorite subjects were

IT'S A FACT!

Sod houses were both easy and cheap to build. They were cool in the summer and warm in the winter. But when it rained, the sod house would leak. Sod houses also attracted insects and snakes.

A Nebraska family poses in front of their sod house.

English, history, and poetry. The Ingalls family was sure their life was settled in Walnut Grove. Pa grew a good wheat crop, which was sure to bring in good money at the market. But then trouble came.

Plunk! something hit Laura's head and fell to the ground. She looked down and saw the largest grasshopper she had ever seen. . . . The cloud was hailing grasshoppers. The cloud was grasshoppers. Their bodies hid the sun and made darkness. . . .

Laura tried to beat them off. Their claws clung to her skin and her dress. They looked at her with bulging eyes, turning their heads this way and that. Mary ran screaming into the house. Grasshoppers covered the ground.

As the grasshoppers moved in on the crops, Laura's mother slammed shut windows and doors in the house. Pa hitched up the horses. He drove the wagon around the wheat field, pitching hay into tiny piles. Ma ran from the barn with a pitchfork and lit the hay into small fires. They hoped the

smoke would chase away the grasshoppers, but it didn't. The Ingalls family sat in their house, helpless, while the insects ate their crop.

The next year, Pa tried to grow wheat again, but the grasshoppers returned and ate the crop. In 1876, they moved farther west, to Burr Oak, Iowa, where Pa's friend owned a hotel. For a while, Laura and her family lived in the hotel. Ma and Pa helped manage the business. Later, the Ingalls rented rooms over a grocery. Soon, they moved to a little brick house outside of town.

Restless and homesick for their friends in Walnut Grove, the Ingalls returned to Minnesota in the summer of 1877. The family lived in town. Pa supported the family by doing carpentry and odd jobs.

Big and Little Problems

Grasshoppers weren't the only problem for farming families. Pioneers had to deal with other natural disasters, such as floods, tornadoes, and dust storms. In the summer of 1859, a drought started. This long period without rain lasted until the fall. Farmers had no water to feed their crops. Thousands of pioneers abandoned their land because their crops had died.

Two years later, tragedy struck again. Mary, at the age of fifteen, had a stroke (a broken blood vessel in the brain). The stroke left her blind. The family wanted to send her to a school for blind people, but they couldn't afford it. Later in the year, Aunt Docia from Wisconsin visited the Ingalls. She had good news. Her husband worked with the Chicago Northwestern railroad company. He wanted to offer Pa a job as a railroad manager in Dakota Territory (modern North and South Dakota). Chicago Northwestern needed smart, strong workers to manage the work crews. When the railroad work ended, Pa filed a claim for 160 acres of free land. The Ingalls were among the first residents of the new town of De Smet in Dakota Territory.

TEACHING, MARRYING, WRITING

In 1881, the Ingalls had saved enough money to send Mary to a school for the blind in Vinton, Iowa. Laura wanted to help Mary too. At the age of fifteen, Laura earned a teaching certificate. She was hired to teach at the Bouchie School, about twelve miles from De Smet. Laura was excited to be earning money for the first time. She would be able to help her sister too.

Laura lived with the Bouchie family, who ran the school. But she was very homesick. Almanzo Wilder was a twenty-four-year-old farmer and the brother of one of Laura's former teachers. He offered to drive Laura home each weekend to be with her parents. Every weekend for three years, often in bad weather, Almanzo picked up Laura in his horse and buggy and took her home.

Sitting side by side on the long drives to De Smet, the two fell in love. They married on August 25, 1885. Laura gave birth to a daughter, Rose, on December 5, 1886.

Laura married Almanzo Wilder in 1885.

Almanzo and Laura's early years were difficult. Droughts and hail killed their crops. Almanzo got a disease called diphtheria, which left him disabled. In August 1889, their second child was born, but the baby died soon after birth. They experienced still more misfortune when a kitchen accident burned their house down.

Laura was used to hard times. She had a strong spirit. She was also used to moving. For a time, the family lived with Almanzo's parents in Spring Valley, Minnesota. Then they moved to Westville, Florida, and in 1892, they headed back to De Smet. On July 17, 1894, the Wilders left South Dakota for the last time. They purchased a home in Mansfield, Missouri, a town in the Ozark Mountains. They called their new home Rocky Ridge Farm.

In her peaceful later years, Laura began writing. At first, she wrote articles for magazines such as the *Missouri Ruralist*. Her daughter Rose, also a writer, encouraged her mother to write about her childhood memories. In 1930, Laura wrote her autobiography, *Pioneer Girl,* but she couldn't find anyone to publish it. With Rose's help, Laura rewrote the book, creating *Little House*

in the Big Woods. The book was an instant success. She went on to write several more books. Together they became known as the Little House series, including *Little House on the Prairie, On the Banks of Plum Creek,* and *The Long Winter.*

IT'S A FACT!

A popular TV show, *Little House on the Prairie,* was based on Laura's books. It ran for ten years in the 1970s and 1980s.

Laura and Almanzo are pictured in front of their house in Missouri in the 1930s. In her sixties, Laura wrote her stories about growing up on the American frontier.

Almanzo died on October 23, 1949. And
Laura followed on February 10, 1957. She died at
home at Rocky Ridge Farm in Missouri. She was
ninety years old.

Laura's books continue to charm readers in the
twenty-first century. They are also a valuable way
to understand life in the United States during the
1800s. Laura Ingalls Wilder lived through hard
times during her childhood, yet she appreciated her
experiences. Near the end of her life, in a letter to
her readers, Laura wrote, "It is still best to be
honest and truthful; to make the most of what we
have; to be happy with simple pleasures and to be
cheerful and have courage when things go wrong."

CHAPTER 3
WOMEN WHO MADE THEIR MARK

(Above)
Known as
"Little Sure
Shot," Annie
Oakley
hardly ever
missed her
shot.

IN THE MID-1800S, hundreds of thousands of people moved westward. Most of the travelers were men, but some women came too. Many women traveled with their husbands and children. One of every ten female travelers was a single woman. They were looking for new adventures and new chances for a better life. Some of these female travelers became legends.

PHOEBE ANN MOSEY

Phoebe Ann Mosey was born in a wooden shack in Darke County, Ohio, on August 13, 1860. Phoebe Ann had thick brown hair and blue gray eyes.

When Phoebe Ann (known as Annie) was born, she had four sisters, Mary Jane, Lydia, Elizabeth, and Sarah Ellen. Soon a brother, John, and two more sisters, Emily and Hulda, joined the Mosey family.

The large family lived on a small farm in the wilderness. The Moseys were very poor. Annie's father was a hunter. He fed his family by hunting small game animals with a gun called a muzzle loader. Annie liked to play outdoors with her brother and explore the forest near her home.

On February 11, 1866, when Annie was five years old, her father died of pneumonia. Her mother was very sad. She was also afraid. How would she support eight children by herself?

IT'S A FACT!

Most writers have recorded the family name as Moses. According to the Annie Oakley Foundation, however, historical records show the name as Mosey.

Annie's brother, John, hunted small game to help feed the family. Annie usually went along and begged her brother to let her shoot. When she was eight, she shot a gun for the first time. "I know we stuffed in enough powder to kill a buffalo," remembered Annie, who shot a rabbit on her first try. But she didn't know that the gun would "kick" (spring back) when it was fired. "I got the rabbit but my nose was broken," she said.

Life just seemed to get harder for the Mosey family. Annie's oldest sister, Mary Jane, died from tuberculosis, a serious lung disease. Annie's mother sold the family cow to pay the doctor and funeral bills. To support her family, she worked as a midwife, helping women deliver their babies. Soon she met a new man and remarried. But her new husband died in an accident shortly after the marriage.

A NEW LIFE

Annie's mother was broke and desperate. She couldn't afford to feed all her children. In 1870, she gave her youngest child, Hulda, to a neighbor family to raise the child as their own. Soon ten-year-old Annie had to leave home. Her mother sent

Annie's mother sent her to live and work at the Darke County Infirmary *(above)*. In the 1800s, young children were sent away to work. They brought in money that was needed at home.

her to the Darke County Infirmary. The infirmary was a home for elderly, orphaned, and mentally ill people. In exchange for room and board, Annie's job was to help with the younger children there. Annie's mother knew the people who ran the infirmary, Samuel and Nancy Edington. She knew that her daughter would be in good care.

At the infirmary, Nancy Edington took a special liking to Annie. She brought her to live with her own family. Nancy also taught Annie to sew. Annie quickly became a skilled seamstress. Annie

liked the Edingtons, but she missed her home in the country. "I was homesick for the fairy places," she said, "the green moss, the big toadstools, the wild flowers, the bees, the rough grouse, the baby rabbits, the squirrels and the quail."

In 1875, when Annie was fifteen years old, her mother asked her to come home. She had recently remarried and was building a new house. Annie was happy. Finally, she would be with her family again.

Before returning home, Annie stopped at the Katzenberger brothers' grocery store on Main Street. Annie had shopped at the store many times for the infirmary. She knew that the Katzenbergers bought fresh game from local hunters. Annie explained that she was going to live with her family in the woods in the north. She planned to hunt and trap game. She asked if the brothers would buy the game she shot. The Katzenbergers agreed, and Annie was in business.

Annie shot and trapped small game such as squirrels and rabbits. She also hunted birds, including quail, grouse, and wild turkeys. She always hit her targets in the head. That way, she figured, the animals suffered less. Annie had another rule. "I always preferred taking my shot

when the game was on the move," she said. "It gave them a fair chance, and made me quick of eye and hand."

Annie's stepfather, Joseph Shaw, was a mail carrier. He made two trips a week to Greenville. On those days, Annie packed up the game she had shot, and her stepfather carried it to the Katzenbergers' store. The store owners then shipped the meat to hotels and restaurants in Dayton and Cincinnati (big cities in Ohio). Diners often praised the meat Annie delivered. They said it tasted better. Because she was careful to hit the game in the head, no lead shot (small lead pellets fired from a shotgun) was left in the meat.

IT'S A FACT!
Annie was a natural gun shooter. She had an almost perfect eye, and she rarely missed a shot. "I don't know how I acquired the skill, but I suppose I was born with it," she said.

Annie gave all the money she earned to her mother. "Oh, how my heart leaped with joy," she recalled, "as I handed the money to mother and told her that I had saved enough from my trapped game to pay [the house] off!"

MEETING FRANK BUTLER

In the late 1800s, people who could shoot well were highly respected. Shooting competitions became popular. Skilled shooters, called sharpshooters, could earn a good living. They competed against other shooters for prize money and for showing off their skills.

In November 1875, in Oakley, Ohio, fifteen-year-old Annie Mosey lifted her gun to her side. A friend had suggested that she try her skill against a professional sharpshooter. Annie had never competed with an expert marksman before, but she was ready. She hollered, "Pull!" and the referee released an excited brown pigeon. Annie calmly took aim and fired. *Ka-boom!* She hit the bird. The crowd that had gathered to watch the shooting match cheered. Annie smiled. Her opponent, Frank Butler, didn't know what to say.

"I almost dropped dead when a little slim girl in short dresses stepped out to the mark with me," Butler said. "I was a beaten man the moment she appeared, for I was taken off guard."

Butler, twenty-four, was a traveling exhibition shooter from the eastern United States. He was charming and easy to get along with. He had

Frank Butler *(right)*, a champion sharpshooter, was impressed with Annie's skills.

brown hair and a mustache. He was known as a "crack shot," a champion sharpshooter who had invented several shooting stunts. When he passed through the Oakley area, near Cincinnati, a friend had invited him to compete against an unknown local shooter.

"Never did anyone make more impossible shots than did that little girl," Butler said after the match. "She killed 23 and I killed 21. It was her

first big match—my first defeat." Although Butler
didn't like to lose, he was impressed. "Right then
and there I fell in love with her and I wanted to
make her mine," he said.

Soon Frank left town to travel with the Sells
Brothers Circus. But he
couldn't forget about
Annie. Within a year,
Frank had won the heart
of young Annie Mosey.
On August 23, 1876, ten
days after Annie's
sixteenth birthday, the
couple married.

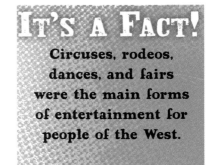

IT'S A FACT!
Circuses, rodeos,
dances, and fairs
were the main forms
of entertainment for
people of the West.

For a few years, Annie stayed home while
Frank traveled with his shooting partner, John
Graham. In 1882, Annie joined the Graham and
Butler act on tour, but she wasn't part of the show.
Then on May 1 that year, Graham was ill and
Annie filled in for him, assisting Frank with his act.
Annie held targets for Frank to shoot. At one point
in the show, Annie held an object that Frank just
couldn't shoot. He tried many times, but he kept
missing. The crowd grew restless. A large man in
the audience yelled, "Let the girl shoot!"

Annie hadn't practiced the shot, but she wasn't going to be laughed at. She took the gun and fired. She hit the target! The crowd cheered. Frank again took the gun, but nobody wanted to see him shoot. The crowd yelled for Annie.

After that day, Annie was the star of the show. Soon Annie and Frank created their own traveling act. Frank wasn't jealous that people liked Annie so much. He was proud of her.

Annie always wore a dress when she performed.

ANNIE OAKLEY

Annie thought she needed a stage name. Because she and Frank had met in Oakley, Ohio, she decided she would be Annie Oakley. They called their act Butler and Oakley.

Frank taught Annie the stunts he knew. He helped her while she practiced. He threw balls in the air for her to shoot or sat still while she shot an apple off the top of his head. Frank also showed

Annie practices shooting glass balls thrown into the air. A Native American man in the show watches her.

Annie how to entertain an audience. She learned how to build excitement by making each stunt a little more difficult than the one before it. Frank helped Annie in another way too. He taught her to read and write.

Frank and Annie traveled throughout the Midwest by train. They performed their shooting act in many theaters. Usually they stayed in cheap hotels. They kept all of their belongings in a trunk, which they hauled with them wherever they went. Sometimes Butler and Oakley played with other traveling acts, such as the Sells Brothers Circus.

LITTLE SURE SHOT

In March 1884, Annie and Frank performed at the Olympic Theater in Saint Paul, Minnesota. One man in the audience loved Annie's act. Chief Sitting Bull was famous for his role in the 1876 Battle of the Little Bighorn. In this battle, Sioux Indians killed Colonel George Armstrong Custer and his U.S. Army troops. Sitting Bull was deeply moved by Annie's talent. He thought her ability with a gun was amazing. He was fascinated by her quiet confidence. He had never seen a woman like her.

Over time, Sitting Bull and Annie became friends. Sitting Bull, who had lost his own daughter a few years earlier, wanted to adopt Annie. Annie accepted. Sitting Bull gave her the Indian name Watanya Cicilia. In the Sioux language, this means "Little Sure Shot."

Annie stood apart from other shooters. She had the skill and the ability to excite a crowd. Audiences loved her girlish excitement. When she finished her act, she would jump high in the air and click her heels together. "There was magnetism in the way she smiled, curtsied in the footlights, and did that funny little kick as she ran into the wings," said writer Shirl Kasper.

In 1885, Annie joined Buffalo Bill's Wild West show. This popular outdoor show featured a cast of cowboys and Indians. Buffalo Bill's real name was William F. Cody. The performers in Cody's traveling show put on riding, shooting, and roping shows. They acted out wagon train scenes and scenes from western novels, such as Indians chasing stagecoaches.

The show called Annie "the maid of the Western plains." She was the headline (main) act in the show. Frank became her manager and assistant. When Annie came onstage, she waved and blew kisses to the audience. Then she started doing one trick after another. Each stunt was more complex than the last. Annie could shoot with her left hand or her right hand. Sometimes during a show, Annie stopped shooting and set her rifle on the dusty

A poster for Buffalo Bill's Wild West show advertises Annie as the star of the show.

ground. She would circle around the gun for good luck. When she again picked up her gun and shot her target, the thrilled crowd yelled for more.

Annie could shoot a cigarette out of Frank's mouth, hit a dime thrown in the air, shoot the flames off candles while they spun on a wheel, and send a storm of bullets through a playing card. Annie's card-shooting trick was so popular that the name "Annie Oakley" became another term for a

free ticket to the theater. At the time, a free theater
pass had a hole punched in it–just like a playing
card when Annie was done with it!

Annie also liked to do gymnastics, such as
handsprings and cartwheels. She could shoot targets
while standing on a galloping horse or while riding
her bicycle. In one stunt, Frank tossed eleven glass
balls into the air. In just ten seconds, Annie
shattered each ball one by one. She saved her best
trick for last. She rested her rifle on her shoulder
and turned her back to her target. Then looking at
the reflection of the target with the shiny blade of a
pocket knife in her hand, she took aim and fired.
She never missed!

Buffalo Bill's Wild West show played in more
than one hundred cities in a year. The group
traveled all over Europe, Asia, and North and
South America. Annie showed off her amazing
abilities to world leaders in many countries. For a
few years, Annie Oakley was the most famous
woman in the world.

As an adult, Annie never forgot her difficult
childhood years. She found ways to help needy
children. She talked Buffalo Bill into offering a
weekly Orphan Day. On that day, children without

parents got free tickets to the show and they were treated to candy and ice-cream cones.

In 1901, a train carrying the Wild West performers crashed in North Carolina. The accident left Annie partially paralyzed, ending her sixteen-year career with the Wild West show. Eventually Annie recovered from the accident. In 1912, she toured one last time in a show called the Young Buffalo Wild West.

IT'S A FACT!

The king of the West African country of Senegal saw Annie's act in Paris, France. He liked Annie so much that he tried to buy her from Buffalo Bill. Annie found the offer funny. She politely told the king that she was not for sale.

In her later years, Annie kept busy. She shot in local competitions and taught thousands of women how to use guns. She also gave shooting performances to raise money for charity. The money from the shows went to children's charities and to young women who wanted a college education. Annie helped more than twenty women attend college. On November 3, 1926, in Greenville, Ohio, Annie Oakley died

after a short illness. Just a few weeks later, Frank Butler died too.

THE UNSINKABLE MAGGIE BROWN

Margaret (Maggie) Tobin was born on July 18, 1867, in the small town of Hannibal, Missouri. Her parents, John Tobin and Johanna Collins Tobin, were poor, hard working immigrants from Ireland. Maggie had three sisters and two brothers. The children went to school in the home of their aunt, Mary O'Leary. Maggie's father worked at the Hannibal Gas Works. But the Tobin family still struggled to pay the bills.

Maggie's childhood home *(above)* had three rooms—a bedroom, a kitchen, and a front room.

In 1880, when Maggie was thirteen, she finished her studies and found work at Garth's Tobacco Factory. Her job was to strip leaves off tobacco plants. She didn't mind working, but she wished for a better life. She dreamed of being rich someday. And she wanted adventure.

In 1886, she boarded a train to Leadville, Colorado, where her older sister and brother were living. This western boomtown was nicknamed the Greatest Mining Camp in the World. The town was full of activity. New settlers arrived daily from all over the world, hoping to make their fortune in the mines.

Maggie eventually got work sewing curtains and carpets. Her coworkers liked her. She was smart and fun to talk to. Soon nineteen-year-old Margaret met someone special at a church picnic.

IT'S A FACT!

A famous musical was staged about Maggie Brown. In it, she was called the Unsinkable Molly Brown. The person who wrote the words to the musical changed her name. He thought he could find better rhymes for "Molly" than he could for "Maggie." Margaret Brown never went by the name Molly.

James "J. J." Brown was a tall, handsome Irishman. He was thirteen years older than Maggie. J. J. worked as a foreman (supervisor) in a silver mine. On September 1, 1886, Maggie and J. J. were married. Both J. J. and Maggie wished to continue their education. After their marriage, they took lessons with a tutor in Leadville. Maggie studied literature and music. She also took piano and voice lessons.

On August 30, 1887, Margaret gave birth to her first child, Lawrence Palmer Brown. A second child, Catherine Ellen, was born on July 1, 1889.

STRIKING IT RICH

By 1892, J. J. had become an engineer at the mine. He also became a minor stockholder (part owner) in the Ibex Mining Company, which owned a group of silver mines. A year later, one of the mines struck gold. Instantly, J. J. was a millionaire.

With their new fortune, the Brown family went on a trip to visit friends and family around the country. In 1894, the Browns moved to Denver, Colorado. After working hard for many years, Maggie had seen her get-rich dreams become a

This silver mine in Leadville, Colorado, was the source of
the Browns' money.

reality. Now she had a new goal. She wanted to be
accepted in the "high society" of Denver.

Colorado women had just won the right to
vote in national elections. Maggie had always been
interested in public service and education, so she
joined several women's political clubs in the
Denver area. She soon became active in the
Denver Woman's Press Club. There, she worked
to gain the right to vote for all women in the

United States. In 1898, she was elected to be chairperson of the Art and Literature Committee of the Denver Women's Club.

Maggie enjoyed her role in politics. She especially liked being part of Denver's women's clubs. She also liked seeing her name in the local newspapers. Many people in Denver appreciated Maggie's lively personality. "Mrs. Brown's vivacity and merry disposition is a most refreshing trait in a society woman of her position," wrote the *Denver*

Maggie stayed active in politics throughout her life.

Times, "for in the smart set any disposition to be natural and animated is quite frowned upon."

J. J. was happy in Denver too. He enjoyed his new position as manager of his own mining company. But the Browns had problems in their personal life. The couple found that they had less and less in common. While Maggie enjoyed Denver's social life, J. J. was more comfortable in his mining career. Maggie shocked the community (as well as her family) when she divorced J. J. In the early 1900s, divorce was very uncommon. She and J. J. agreed on Maggie keeping quite a lot of money. She had become a very wealthy woman.

It's a Fact!

Between 1870 and 1900, more divorces took place in the West than they did in any other part of the United States.

TITANIC VOYAGE

Maggie had enough money to travel the world. In April 1912, Maggie boarded a huge luxury ocean liner called *Titanic.* She was on her way home from Great Britain. Aboard the *Titanic,* Maggie continued to do things her own way. She was

In 1912, the *Titanic* was the world's largest ship. Its first trip was to be from Southampton, England, to New York City.

traveling alone. Many people didn't feel a lady should travel without a man at her side. But Maggie didn't care what people thought.

Maggie was one of more than twenty-two hundred passengers aboard the grand ship on its first voyage. At the time, *Titanic* was the largest ship ever built. It was called "unsinkable."

Shortly after 11:30 P.M. on April 14, crew member Frederick Fleet was standing up high at the front of the ship. In the dark night, Fleet spotted a dark object set against the starry sky. At first, he didn't know what he was seeing. Quickly, he realized. A huge iceberg lay in the ship's path!

Fleet rang the warning bell three times. In the minutes that followed, *Titanic*'s crew tried to steer the ship away from the iceberg. But the warning had come too late. The iceberg scraped the starboard (right) side of the bow (front of the ship). It tore a long hole in the ship. The crew knew that the ship would sink quickly.

The captain ordered the crew to prepare the lifeboats. But *Titanic* had only twenty lifeboats, enough to save about half the people on board. The captain knew that many people were about to lose their lives. A few moments later, two crewmen helped Maggie—and twenty-three other passengers—onto lifeboat Number 6. Two of the passengers were *Titanic* crew members, lookout Frederick Fleet and quartermaster Robert Hichens.

Together the men slowly rowed away from the sinking ship. With only two men rowing, the lifeboat was moving very slowly. Maggie didn't see why the women of the boat couldn't help. She took hold of an oar and asked another woman to grab another oar. The two women rowed hard. The lifeboat began to move faster.

The lifeboat passengers were cold and afraid. Hichens was certain that they were doomed. He said

that their lifeboat wouldn't be found and that they would all surely freeze to death or drown. Finally, Maggie asked him to stop scaring everyone. "Keep it to yourself if you feel that way!" she said. "We have a smooth sea and a fighting chance!"

Maggie tried to be brave, especially when she heard a great rumbling sound coming from *Titanic.* The ship was sinking fast. As the ship went down, the passengers of lifeboat Number 6 sat and stared, their eyes wide with horror. Each of them had a loved one or a friend on the ship. Maggie was frightened and sad, but she wasn't ready to give up hope. Her hands were bleeding from the rowing, but she rowed even harder. She told others on the boat that rowing would keep them warm.

A couple of hours later, a ship came into view. Maggie was happy–they would be rescued! At about 6:00 A.M., lifeboat Number 6 arrived at the *Carpathia,* the ship that was waiting to rescue them. It took nearly five hours for the lifeboat passengers to be rescued. When the twenty lifeboats arrived at the rescue ship, most of the survivors were so cold and tired that they needed help making it aboard.

HELPING THE SURVIVORS

Maggie Brown's efforts to help her fellow *Titanic* passengers didn't stop when survivors reached the safety of the *Carpathia*. Many survivors had lost loved ones in the tragedy. Others had lost their money and possessions. Before the *Carpathia* reached New York, Maggie had helped form the Survivors Committee and raised nearly $10,000 for survivors and their families. As head of the Survivors Committee, Maggie presented a silver cup to Captain Arthur Rostron of the *Carpathia* on May 29, 1912. She also gave a medal to each crew member.

Maggie Brown presents a silver cup to the captain of the *Carpathia*. She was rewarding him for his efforts in saving passengers of the *Titanic*.

Maggie Brown continued her interest in politics. In 1914, she ran for the U.S. Senate—eight years before all U.S. women had won the right to vote. Although she didn't win the election, she was one of the first women in the United States to run for political office.

Maggie also helped set up an international woman's rights conference in 1914 in Newport, Rhode Island. Women from all over the world attended the conference. During World War I (1914–1918), Maggie worked with the American Committee for Devastated France, helping U.S. and French soldiers. In 1932, Maggie was awarded the French Legion of Honor for her "overall good citizenship." Margaret Tobin Brown died of a brain tumor on October 26, 1932, in New York. She was buried next to J. J., who had died ten years earlier, on Long Island, New York.

CHAPTER 4

FEMALE OUTLAWS AND REBELS

THE WILD WEST was informal. Women adapted their clothing to their work. For example, some women cut several inches off the skirts of their dresses so they wouldn't drag in the mud. They didn't dress fashionably either. They spent their days, often alone, cooking, cleaning, farming, and sewing.

(Above) Two women brand a cow. Most women in the West wore dresses, even when they worked.

71

Yet most of the married women in the West still had ideas about what was feminine and unfeminine behavior. The women of Deadwood, South Dakota, where Calamity Jane lived, thought she was one of the most unfeminine creatures ever. She rebelled against their ideas of what made a woman worthwhile. And she wasn't the only one who rebelled.

CALAMITY JANE

This time, Calamity Jane (Martha Jane Cannary) had gone too far. The ladies of Deadwood were going to do something about it. Not only did Calamity dress like a man, drink too much, and get in fights—now she was working as a bartender in a saloon! The ladies agreed that no woman should be doing that job. A lady belonged in the home, caring for her family. An unmarried woman like Calamity should make a living as a schoolteacher or a seamstress.

The women of Deadwood saw it as their job to help Calamity. First, they wanted to cut her stringy hair. They didn't like the way she wore it down, messy and unwashed. "They came into the saloon with a horse whip and shears to cut my

Calamity Jane shocked the women of Deadwood, Dakota Territory, by dressing and acting like a man.

hair," recalled Calamity. But Calamity wouldn't let them. "I jumped off the bar into their midst and before they could say sickem I had them bowling!" Fearing for their lives, the townswomen ran off. They did not bother Calamity again.

Calamity Jane was a legendary character of both fiction and real life. She was the brave heroine of

Wild West novels and an adventurer in the Black Hills of South Dakota. She was tall and strong. She carried a gun in a holster on her hip. She swore, chewed tobacco, and drank heavily. Her face was dark and lined from spending many years outdoors in the sun. She always looked older than she really was.

Stories about Calamity's life differ. The truth is hard to know because she liked to make up stories about herself. She wrote some of these stories in her autobiography. Fiction writers also came up with stories about Calamity in western novels. This much is certain—Calamity Jane lived her life boldly. She did as she pleased, and she didn't let many people get close to her.

IT'S A FACT!

Some people believe that there were three Calamity Janes. During her career, newspapers reported she was in several different places around the West.

NOT LIKE MOST GIRLS

According to her, Calamity Jane was born Martha Jane Cannary on May 1, 1852, in Princeton, Missouri. Her father, Robert, and her mother, Charlotte, had grown up in Ohio. Martha was

their first child. Later, she had two brothers and
three sisters.

Martha wasn't like most girls of her day. She
wasn't interested in cooking, sewing, and other
homemaking skills. She preferred to spend time
outdoors with her father and brothers.

"As a child I always had a fondness for
adventure and outdoor exercise," she wrote in
her autobiography. She especially loved to ride
horses. "I began to ride at an early age and
continued to do so until I became an expert rider
being able to ride the most vicious and stubborn
of horses, in fact the greater portion of my life in
early times was spent in this manner."

In 1865, Martha's parents moved the family
west to Virginia City, Montana. Like many
families, they hoped for a better life in the new
settlement. Traveling by covered wagon, the
family met with many difficulties along the way.
But thirteen-year-old Martha enjoyed the
adventure. She liked being able to ride her pony
every day, and the men taught her to shoot
and hunt.

Later, Calamity Jane remembered her travels
west. "While on the way the greater portion of my

time was spent in hunting along with the men and hunters of the party, in fact I was at all times with the men when there was excitement and adventures to be had."

Five months later, the Cannarys finally reached Virginia City. In the spring of 1867, the family moved to Utah. On the way there, in Blackfoot, Montana, Martha's mother became ill and died. The rest of the family arrived in Salt Lake City, Utah, that summer. Soon Martha's father became ill and died. The Cannary children had no choice but to try to make it on their own. They continued their journey. In May 1868, they arrived in Fort Bridger, Wyoming. Sixteen-year-old Martha hunted for food and took odd jobs to help support her brothers and sisters.

CHILDREN AT WORK

In the West, children were often regarded as little adults. They were expected to be mature, brave, and able to help the family in every possible way. Each member of the family, including children as young as three, was expected to help with housekeeping. Girls typically cooked, cleaned, and took care of smaller children. Boys usually worked in the fields and took care of animals. But both boys and girls took on whatever work was needed, no matter what their gender.

CALAMITY

By this time, Martha had become an excellent rider and sharpshooter. She wanted to put her skills to good use. Colonel George Armstrong Custer of the U.S. Army needed scouts in his campaign to fight the Sioux, Cheyenne, and other Indians on the Great Plains. "When I joined Custer I donned the uniform of a soldier, it was a bit awkward at first, but I soon got to be perfectly at home in men's clothes," Martha wrote.

Calamity was a scout for Colonel Custer's troops.

According to Calamity Jane's autobiography, she earned her famous nickname in 1873, on one of her missions for the army. At Goose Creek, Wyoming, under the command of Captain Egan, Martha Jane and her fellow soldiers were heading back to their military camp one day. They were attacked by a large group of Sioux Indians. Captain Egan was shot and started to fall from his horse. Martha Jane circled back. With great effort, she pulled Egan onto her horse and rode him safely back to the army camp. When the captain recovered from his injuries, he said to Martha Jane, "I name you Calamity Jane, the heroine of the plains."

Most historians do not believe Calamity Jane's account of how she got her nickname. Biographer J. Leonard Jennewein wrote, "There is no [proven] version of how Calamity acquired the name 'Calamity.' The story as given in her autobiography is known to be false. All we can say is that she lived in an adventurous time and place and that someone tagged her with the name 'Calamity' and it stuck."

In the 1870s, Calamity Jane worked in the Black Hills of South Dakota. Her job was to

protect gold and silver miners and settlers from Indian attacks. She also worked as a messenger between U.S. Army camps. Her duties included swimming across the Platte River to deliver important messages and then riding, wet and cold, ninety miles on her horse.

Calamity didn't like to stay anywhere for long. She soon headed for Fort Laramie, Wyoming, where she met William Hickok, better known as Wild Bill Hickok. The two traveled together to Deadwood, Dakota Territory, arriving in June 1876.

IT'S A FACT!

Calamity later said that she and Wild Bill had a romance. But this may have been one of her tall tales. Hickok said that he and Calamity Jane were just friends.

Wild Bill Hickok

While Calamity was often wild, she had a kind and generous side too. Many people in Deadwood had good things to say about her. "She was outstanding, that woman was . . . if she had a chance to [help] somebody . . . out of a tight place she was right there," remembered Charles Haas, who knew Calamity. "Lots of us . . . knew the better side of Calamity. But then, you know, she

A scene from Lower Main Street in Deadwood, Dakota Territory, in 1877.

would go to these bawdy [rough] houses and
dance halls and it was 'whoopee' and soon she
was drunk and then, well, things just sort of went
haywire with old Calamity!"

On August 2, 1876, Wild Bill Hickok was
playing poker in Deadwood when he was shot in
the back of the head by
Jack McCall. Calamity
said that she went after
McCall with a meat
cleaver when she heard
the news. But nobody
knows if that story is true.

While it is hard to
know what was true about
Calamity Jane, we do
know that she was a hero
at least once. In 1876, a
disease called smallpox swept through Deadwood.
Hundreds of people became ill. Because the
disease couldn't be cured at that time, most
people were afraid to help the victims. Dr.
Babcock, the town's only doctor, remembered
how Calamity risked her life to care for dying
miners. He also recalled that she cared for a

IT'S A FACT!
When Wild Bill
Hickok was killed
playing poker, he
was holding aces and
eights in his hand.
Ever since, poker
players have called
that hand the "dead
man's hand."

young boy named Charles Robinson, who recovered because of her help.

LIFE AFTER DEADWOOD

Calamity left Deadwood in the fall of 1877. Over the next few years, she searched for gold, drove mule trains and, for a while, owned a cattle ranch. All the while, she continued to drink heavily.

In 1884, she went to Texas. In El Paso, thirty-two-year-old Calamity met Clinton Burk. The couple married in August 1885. "As I thought I had traveled through life long enough alone and thought it was about time to take a partner for the rest of my days," Calamity wrote in her autobiography. (As with many aspects of her life, however, this marriage is questioned by some historians.)

Calamity and Clinton remained in Texas until 1889, when they moved to Boulder, Colorado. There, they kept a hotel for a few years. In the fall of 1895, Calamity returned to Deadwood with her husband.

Calamity Jane had been away for many years, but the people of Deadwood had not forgotten her. She had become a legend in the town's history. She

was known as the daring "woman scout" of the
Black Hills. Calamity enjoyed the attention, and she
earned a few dollars selling copies of her life story.
Promoters from the eastern United States, traveling
through Deadwood, asked her to appear in Wild
West shows in eastern cities.

Calamity enjoyed being a western celebrity.
But her years of heavy drinking had taken their
toll on her health. In July 1903, she became ill.
On August 1, Calamity died at the age of fifty-one.
Her undertaker was Charles Robinson. She had
nursed himback to health during the Deadwood
smallpox epidemic.

John Sohn, a longtime Deadwood shoemaker,
described Calamity's
funeral: "There was an
awful lot of people in [the
funeral parlor]. I seen the
picture they took; they
had her propped up
kinda, in a sitting position.
She looked purty good,
Old Calamity did."

IT'S A FACT!
A citizen of
Deadwood noted that
all the men who
carried Calamity
Jane's casket during
her funeral were
bartenders.

Not everyone who
visited Calamity in the funeral parlor had good

intentions. Some townswomen brought in scissors and clipped locks of her hair. A friend put a stop to that by building a wire screen around her body.

On the day of Calamity's funeral, people traveled from distant towns to pay their respects to the Black Hills legend. The people of Deadwood showed their respect for the wild-natured frontier woman. They granted Calamity Jane her dying wish and buried her next to her hero, Wild Bill Hickok.

Calamity Jane tips her hat in front of Wild Bill Hickok's grave. She would later be buried next to him.

Famous stagecoach robber Pearl Hart (left)

PEARL HART

Pearl Hart could make a claim that no other woman—or man—could make. She was the first-known stagecoach robber in Arizona Territory.

Pearl Hart was born in 1871 in Ontario, Canada. She ran away from home when she was seventeen and ended up in Arizona. From that point on, Pearl was trouble.

In 1889, she met a miner named Joe Boot. Together the couple shared a life of crime, working as a team. Pearl first tricked men to come to her

room by promising them romance. But once the men were in her room, Joe knocked them out and took their money.

For more excitement and money, Pearl and Joe decided to rob stagecoaches, which carried passengers and their money. To hide her identity, Pearl cut her hair and wore men's clothing. But Pearl and Joe weren't smart enough. After they robbed a Globe, Arizona, stagecoach of $400, they took off on their horses–and got lost.

The next morning, the sheriff found them asleep beneath some trees. Pearl was arrested and put on trial. Luckily for her, she was a good actress.

CHARLEY PARKHURST

Charley Parkhurst drove a stagecoach for the California Stage Lines in the 1850s. He had a scarred face and a missing eye. His cheekbone was out of place. He dressed in dirty, oversized pants. He liked to smoke and chew tobacco.

Until December 19, 1879, the day Charley died, no one knew that Charley Parkhurst was actually a woman. A local reporter wrote, "It could scarcely be believed by persons who knew Charley Parkhurst for a quarter of a century." Charley had been born Charlotte Parkhurst. Charlotte was placed in an orphanage at an early age. She soon put on boys' clothes and ran away. From then on, she pretended to be a man.

She told the jury that she had robbed the stagecoach because her mother in Canada was ill and needed the money. The jury believed her. Pearl was released, only to be arrested again a short time later for unlawfully carrying a gun.

Pearl was sent to the Yuma Territorial Prison in Arizona. She was the first woman to be sent to the prison. She later became the only prisoner to become pregnant while held there. The scandal served Pearl well. The only two men who had been alone with her in her cell were the governor of Arizona and a Christian minister. Pearl was released.

In her later years, Pearl performed as a stagecoach-robbing outlaw for a short time with Buffalo Bill's Wild West show. Later, she returned to Arizona, where she married a rancher and lived a crime-free life.

CATTLE ANNIE AND LITTLE BRITCHES

In 1894, Annie McDougall and Jennie Stevens stood back and watched the handsome cowboys at a dance in Guthrie, Oklahoma. "Know who they are?" asked a friend. When the teenage girls shook their heads, he said, "That's Bill Doolin and some of his boys."

Cattle Annie *(left)* and Little Britches *(right)* were teenaged outlaws.

The Doolin gang–Red Buck, Charley Pierce, and Bill Doolin–was known for its daring adventures. The boys looked wild and dangerous. They impressed Annie, who was seventeen, and Jennie, sixteen. That night, the girls decided to run away from home and become famous outlaws with the Doolin boys.

The gang hired the teens as lookouts. Soon the young women were known as Cattle Annie and Little Britches. When the Doolin gang broke up, the girls made their way the best they could. They

sold whiskey to the Osage Indians and stole cattle.
U.S. marshals finally caught them at a farmhouse
near Pawnee, Oklahoma.

Cattle Annie and Little Britches were sent to
a prison in Boston, Massachusetts. They quickly
became celebrities. Crowds formed outside the
prison, hoping to catch a glimpse of the
Oklahoma Girl Bandits. After serving two years in
prison, however, Annie and Jennie didn't
think the outlaw life seemed so great anymore.
Annie married and settled down. Jennie moved to
New York to find work. Two years later, she died
of tuberculosis.

THE BANDIT QUEEN

Although her wealthy parents had raised Myra
Belle Shirley to be ladylike, the woman who
became Belle Starr was born to be a rebel. With
her big brown eyes and dark hair, Belle was
described as mean as a rattlesnake. She liked to
drink and swear.

Belle was born in 1848. When she was
eighteen, living with her parents in Scyne, Texas,
Belle met a man named Cole Younger. Younger was
attractive and dangerous. He was an outlaw and a

close friend of the famous bank robber Jesse James. Belle ran off with Younger and joined his outlaw gang.

A few months later, Belle returned home. She was pregnant. In 1867, her daughter, Pearl Younger, was born. Belle called the little girl Rosie.

Belle didn't stay unmarried for long. When she was twenty, she met James Reed. Her parents approved of the match at first. Reed had been a soldier in the Civil War (1861–1865), fighting for the Confederacy (the South). But Reed was an outlaw too. Like Younger, he was a friend of the James brothers.

Belle married Jim Reed in 1868, and they soon had a son, Ed. While Belle loved her children, she also liked living a wild life. Usually dressed as a man, Belle robbed several stagecoaches and banks throughout the West. Quickly, she earned the nickname the Bandit Queen. She also stole horses. Although she was arrested many times, she always was able to get out of trouble. She was sent to jail once but quickly managed to talk her way out.

In 1880, Belle married Sam Starr, a Native American of the Cherokee tribe. The couple settled on Sam's tribal land along the Canadian River in

Belle rides with her husband, Sam Starr (right).

Oklahoma. They called the place Younger's Bend
in honor of Belle's first love, Cole Younger.

Belle lived happily on her land with Sam,
Pearl (then thirteen) and Ed (about ten). She
enjoyed her privacy and didn't miss the
company of other women. "So long have I been
[away] from the society of women (whom I
thoroughly detest), that I thought it would be
irksome to be in their midst," Belle once told a
newspaper reporter.

Although she liked her home, Belle wasn't
quite ready to settle down. In 1883, Belle and Sam
were arrested for horse theft. Newspapers around
the country carried news of the event, and Belle
was nicknamed the Petticoat Terror of the Plains.
During Belle's trial, her children were sent to live
with friends. Belle and Sam were given nine
months in jail. There, Belle became friends with the
warden (the man who ran the jail) and his wife.
Belle had an easy time in jail and was released
early. Sam, meanwhile, served his full sentence,
working at heavy labor.

Belle wasn't ready to change her ways. When
Sam got out of jail, the pair joined a gang of
horse thieves. In 1886,
when Belle was thirty-
eight, Sam was killed
during an argument at a
friend's party.

When Sam died,
Belle worried that she
would lose her home. She
quickly married another
Cherokee, Jim July. July was a handsome,
educated man of twenty-four. According to tribal

IT'S A FACT!

Belle Starr was a
popular topic for
journalists. Their
readers loved the
image of her as a
romantic criminal.

law, Belle and her new husband could stay on the land at Younger's Bend.

Belle had made too much trouble in her life not to have enemies. On February 3, 1889, at the age of forty-one, she was riding her horse near her home when she was shot in the face and in the back. She fell from her horse, dead.

Two days later, the *Fort Smith Elevator* carried the headline, "BELLE STARR MURDERED FROM AMBUSH BY UNKNOWN PARTIES." No one ever found out who killed her.

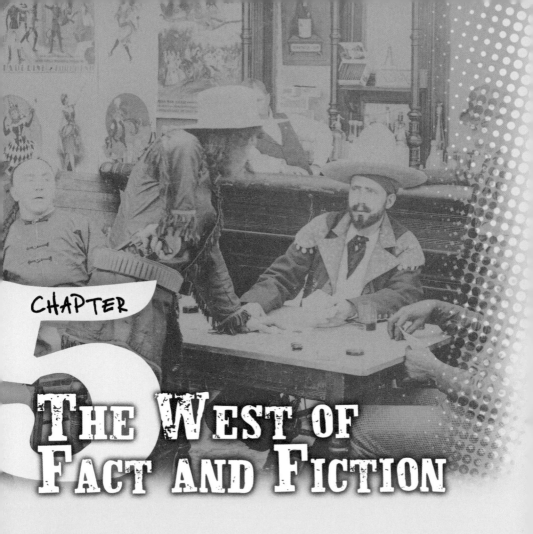

5

THE WEST OF FACT AND FICTION

Many stories about the Wild West play with the truth. Some have been made into movies (above).

IMAGES OF THE WILD WEST are still popular in the United States. People think of tough-talking cowboys and cowgirls, saloon fights, and good guys fighting outlaws. Books, television shows, movies, and plays have told many stories about the West. People remain interested in the true stories as well as the

myths. They love the idea of the frontier and the idea of new land and endless possibilities. In hard economic times, the wish for a better life in the West gave people hope.

That idea has not changed. People still hope and work for better lives for themselves and their families. Many of us like to learn about brave men and women who fight for their beliefs. The heroes of the Wild West are inspiring.

FIRST BOOKS

Even while Calamity Jane and Wild Bill Hickok were alive, readers could buy books about these well-known western figures. The stories were often made up or changed to be more exciting. Calamity Jane enjoyed her fame. She often bragged about her adventures. She was willing to stretch the truth a bit. Historians agree that much of Martha Cannary's autobiography, *Calamity Jane, Written by Herself*, is fiction.

Authors who wrote about women like Calamity Jane, Annie Oakley, and Maggie Brown knew that people liked action and drama. These writers often changed the facts to make a better story. In turn, folk legends were born.

IT'S A FACT!

Three American actresses had great success playing these legendary characters in the movies. Betty Hutton played Annie Oakley in *Annie Get Your Gun*, which came out in 1950. Doris Day played Calamity Jane in a 1953 movie of the same name. Debbie Reynolds starred in the 1964 movie version of *The Unsinkable Molly Brown*.

Gifted sharpshooter Annie Oakley was a star during her lifetime. But she became a legend after her death. Her life has been shown in books, plays, and films, including the popular musical, *Annie Get Your Gun*.

More stories of the West came with the invention of television. In the 1950s, more than thirty western TV shows were on the air. They showed cowboys such as Gene Autry and Roy Rogers. A comedy show called *Annie Oakley and Tagg* included stories about Annie Oakley, most of which were made up.

Perhaps no western woman has had more stories made up about her than Maggie Tobin Brown. In the 1930s, *Denver Post* writer Gene Fowler wrote about her life in a chapter of his novel, *Timberline*. In the book, Maggie is shown as

crude and strange. Fowler made up details, such as how she once hid (and accidentally burned) the family's savings in a stove. Her actions aboard *Titanic*'s lifeboat Number 6 also came from Fowler's imagination. He included a story about how she stripped off all of her expensive clothes and gave them to cold children and old women.

Maggie Brown didn't bother to fix half-truths that people told about her life.

Romance novelist Carolyn Bancroft wrote another story in a 1930s magazine article, which was turned into a popular booklet called *The Unsinkable Mrs. Brown*. Bancroft's story later was the basis for the 1960 Broadway musical, *The Unsinkable Molly Brown*. Playwright Richard Morris said he used the name Molly because it was easier to sing. Morris didn't just make up most of the facts about Brown. He also invented a name for her!

The 1964 movie *The Unsinkable Molly Brown* only made things worse. And Margaret Brown continues to be shown as someone she really wasn't. In James Cameron's 1997 film, *Titanic*, Margaret (once again called Molly) is shown as a loud-mouthed social misfit. In reality, Maggie was a popular society woman.

Although the made-up facts about Margaret Brown's life are interesting and fun, her real-life actions were also amazing. Throughout her life, she worked for human rights. She fought for women's right to vote. She tried to become a U.S. senator. She also supported the temperance movement (a social movement, led mainly by women, to outlaw alcohol) because she wanted to help women who were abused by alcoholic husbands.

TEMPERANCE MOVEMENTS

The movement to prohibit the sale and drinking of alcohol, called the temperance movement, was one of the first women's movements in the West. The National Women's Christian Temperance Union (WCTU) was formed in Cleveland, Ohio, in 1874. It quickly became one of the largest women's organizations in the world. Its president was Frances Elizabeth Caroline Willard, a woman who had helped settle the western frontier. Frances was a tomboy, wore her hair short, and expected to be called Frank.

NEW IMAGES

Brown and other women challenged ideas about women's roles. Annie Oakley proved that a woman could be as good with a gun as a man could. "Her spunky independence and her amazing accomplishments [foretold] a future in which women would emerge from . . . narrow notions of roles and respectability, imprisoned them in absurd clothes, and kept their hair up and their options down," wrote one historian.

Western women showed that a woman's place was not just in the home. She could also be pushing a plow in the field, selling real estate, or working as a doctor, stagecoach driver, or politician. Women throughout the West made firsts

for women everywhere. In 1869, Esther Morris helped win the right to vote for women in Wyoming. Ex-slave Clara Brown traveled to Colorado and became a successful businesswoman. She also started the first Sunday school in Denver.

American women first earned the right to vote in western states. In 1910, these three women in California showed their support for women's voting rights.

Women helped to shape the American frontier.

Calamity Jane and Pearl Hart ignored
stereotypes. Other western travelers, such as Laura
Ingalls Wilder and Virginia Reed, made a
difference in quiet but powerful ways. Bravely, the
women of the Wild West played an important role
in a changing time.

Buffalo Bill's Wild West show: a show-business act first organized by William F. Cody in 1883. It toured the United States and Europe for many years.

California gold rush: the arrival of thousands of people after the discovery of gold in northern California in January 1848. The gold rush lasted from 1848 to 1856.

Homestead Act: a law passed by the U.S. Congress in 1862. It allowed any citizen over the age of twenty-one to get 160 acres of public land by living on it and farming it for five years.

immigrant: a person who moves from a homeland country into a foreign country and settles there

Indian Removal Act: a law passed by the U.S. Congress in 1830. The law gave money for removing and resettling eastern Indians into lands in the West. It granted the president the authority to use force if necessary.

infirmary: a place where sick people are cared for

Jesse James: a U.S. outlaw who led a band that robbed trains and banks in the West in the late 1800s

Legion of Honor: the highest award given by the president of France to civilians (nonmilitary people)

Louisiana Purchase: a huge area that covered the middle of the United States, which the new nation bought from France in 1803

midwife: a person who helps a woman give birth

Native American tribes: the first peoples to live in North, Central, and South America. Thousands of Native Americans were living in the west when white settlers arrived.

pioneer: a person who travels unmapped lands and settles there

stereotype: an overly simple way of viewing a person, a group, or a thing

stockholder: a person who owns a stock, or part, of a company. A stock has value, so it can be used to show how much money a person has.

voting rights: the legal right to choose officials in national, state, and local elections. Women were slowly gaining this right in the late 1800s. Wyoming, Utah, Colorado, and Idaho—all newly settled states of the West—were the first to give this right to women.

western trails: the overland pathways through the unmapped areas of what would become the western United States. Thousands of people followed the Oregon Trail and the California Trail through the Midwest and the Rocky Mountains to reach the Pacific Ocean.

Source Notes

5   J. Leonard Jennewein, *Calamity Jane of the Western Trails* (Huron, SD: Dakota Books, 1953), 32.

15–16   JoAnn Levy, "The Women" *Women in the Gold Rush*, n.d., http://www.goldrush.com/~joann/women.htm (June 27, 2005).

16–17   Ibid.

21   The Lockley Files, Oregon Collection at the University of Oregon Library, Eugene, OR.

24   Oregon Pioneer Association, 19th Annual Reunion, Transaction (Portland: Oregon Pioneer Association, 1891), 42.

26   The Lockley Files, University of Oregon.

27   Virginia R. Murphy, "Across the Plains in the Donner Party," *Century XLII*, 1891, 411.

32   Dee Brown, *The Gentle Tamers: Women of the Old West* (Lincoln: University of Nebraska Press, 1958), 99.

33   Nancy Wilson Ross, *Westward the Women* (San Francisco: North Point Press, 1985), 16.

34   The Lockley Files, University of Oregon.

37   Laura Ingalls Wilder, *On the Banks of Plum Creek* (New York: Harper and Row, 1937), 194.

43   Jennifer Slegg, "Fan Letter Reply by Laura Ingalls Wilder," *The Definitive Laura Ingalls Wilder Pages*, 2000, http://vvv.com/home/jenslegg/misclett.htm (June 27, 2005).

46   Damaine Vonada, "Annie Oakley Was More Than a 'Crack Shot in Petticoats,' " *Smithsonian*, September 1990, 131.

46   Ibid.

48   Glenda Riley, *The Life and Legacy of Annie Oakley* (Norman: University of Oklahoma Press, 1994), 11.

48–49   Shirl Kasper, *Annie Oakley* (Norman: University of Oklahoma Press, 1992), 7.

49   Riley, 12.

49   Ibid.

50   Kasper, 16, 17.

51–52   Ibid.

52   Ibid.

56   Kasper, 22.

64   Kristen Iversen, *Unraveling the Myth: The Story of Molly Brown* (Boulder, CO: Johnson Publishing, 1999), 147.

68   Logan Marshall, *The Sinking of the Titanic* (Seattle: Hara Publishing, 1998), 112.

72–73   Joan Swallow Reiter, *The Women: The Old West* (Alexandria, VA: Time-Life Books, 1978), n.p.

75   Roberta Beed Sollid, *Calamity Jane: A Study in Historical Criticism* (Helena: The Western Press/Montana Historical Society Press 1958), 125.

75–76   Ibid.

77   Ibid., 126.

78   Ibid., 127.

78 Jennewein, 32.

80-81 Ibid., 33.

82 Ibid., 38.

83 Ibid., 33.

86 Floyd D. P. Øydegaard, "She Was a Man!" *Shadows of the Past*, 2003, http://www.sptddog.com/sotp/parkhurst.html (June 27, 2005).

87 James D. Horan and Paul Sann, *Pictorial History of the Wild West* (New York: Crown, 1954), 171.

91 Richard Young and Judy Dockney, *Outlaw Tales: Legends, Myths, and Folklore from America's Middle Border* (Little Rock, AR: August House, 1992), 203.

93 Ibid., 40.

99 Vonada, 131.

Selected Bibliography

Books

Bartley, Paula, and Cathy Loxton. *Plains Women: Women in the American West.* New York: Cambridge University Press, 1991.

Brown, Dee. *The Gentle Tamers: Women of the Old Wild West.* Lincoln: University of Nebraska Press, 1958.

Iversen, Kristen. *Unraveling the Myth: The Story of Molly Brown.* Boulder, CO: Johnson Publishing, 1999.

Jameson, Elizabeth, and Susan Armitage, eds. *Writing the Range: Race, Class and Culture in the Women's West.* Norman: University of Oklahoma Press, 1997.

Jennewein, J. Leonard. *Calamity Jane of the Western Trails.* Huron, SD: Dakota Books, 1953.

Kasper, Shirl. *Annie Oakley.* Norman, OK: University of Oklahoma Press, 1992.

Levy, JoAnn. *They Saw the Elephant: Women in the California Goldrush.* Hamden, CT: Archon Books, 1990.

Miller, John E. *Becoming Laura Ingalls Wilder: The Woman behind the Legend.* Columbia: University of Missouri Press, 1998.

Peavy, Linda, and Ursula Smith. *Pioneer Women: The Lives of Women on the Frontier.* New York: Smithmark Publishers, 1997.

Riley, Glenda. *The Life and Legacy of Annie Oakley.* Norman: University of Oklahoma, 1994.

Seagraves, Anne. *Daughters of the West.* Hayden, ID: Wesanne Publications, 1996.

Sollid, Roberta Beed. *Calamity Jane: A Study in Historical Criticism.* Helena, MT: The Western Press/ Montana Historical Society Press, 1958.

Stewart, Elinore Pruitt. *Letters of a Woman Homesteader.* Boston: Houghton Mifflin, 1982.

WEBSITES

Annie Oakley Foundation
http://www.annieoakleyfoundation.org

My Little House on the Prairie Home Page
http://vvv.com/~jenslegg/index.htm

New Light on the Donner Party
http://www.metrogourmet.com/crossroads/Kjhome.htm

New Perspectives on THE WEST
http://www.pbs.org/weta/thewest/

The Oregon Trail Home Page
http://www.isu.edu/~trinmich/Oregontrail.html

FURTHER READING AND WEBSITES

Alter, Judy. *Wild West Shows: Rough Riders and Sure Shots.* New York: Franklin Watts, 1997.

Bentley, Judith. *Brides, Midwives, and Widows.* New York: Twenty-First Century Books, 1995.

Cobb, Mary. *The Quilt-Block History of Pioneer Days, with Projects Kids Can Make.* Minneapolis: Millbrook Press, 1995.

Faber, Doris. *Calamity Jane: Her Life and Her Legend.* Boston: Houghton Mifflin, 1992.

Ferris, Jeri. *Native American Doctor: The Story of Susan LaFlesche Picotte.* Minneapolis: Carolrhoda Books, Inc., 1991.

Furbee, Mary Rodd. *Outrageous Women of the American Frontier.* New York: John Wiley & Sons, 2002.

Ichord, Loretta Frances. *Skillet Bread, Sourdough, and Vinegar Pie: Cooking in Pioneer Days.* Minneapolis: Millbrook Press, 2003.

Josephson, Judith Pinkerton. *Growing Up in Pioneer America.* Minneapolis: Lerner Publications Company, 2003.

Katz, William Loren. *Black Women of the Old West.* New York: Atheneum Books for Young Readers, 1995.

Ketchum, Liza. *Into a New Country: Eight Remarkable Women of the West.* Boston: Little, Brown, 2000.

Krensky, Stephen. *Shooting for the Moon: The Amazing Life and Times of Annie Oakley.* New York: Farrar, Straus and Giroux, 2001.

Landau, Elaine. *Heroine of the Titanic: The Real Unsinkable Molly Brown.* New York: Clarion Books, 2001.

Macy, Sue. *Bull's Eye: A Photobiography of Annie Oakley.* Washington, DC: National Geographic Society, 2001.

Manheimer, Ann S. *James Beckwourth: Legendary Mountain Man.* Minneapolis: Twenty-First Century Books, 2006.

Markel, Rita J. *Your Travel Guide to American's Old West.* Minneapolis: Lerner Publications Company, 2004.

Miller, Brandon Marie. *Buffalo Gals: Women of the Old West.* Minneapolis: Lerner Publications Company, 1995.

Naden, Corinne J., and Rose Blue. *Belle Starr and the Wild West.* Woodbridge, CT: Blackbirch Press, 2000.

National Women's Hall of Fame
http://www.greatwomen.org/women.php
This site was created by the National Women's Hall of Fame in New York and is dedicated to honoring great women of the United States. Visitors are able to find biographies, as well as information about the nomination process, recent news, and events.

Outlaw Women
http://www.outlawwomen.com
This site has biographies of many women who helped shape U.S. history.

Sanford, William R., and Carl R. Green. *Calamity Jane: Frontier Original.* Springfield, NJ: Enslow Publishers, 1996.

Sigerman, Harriet. *Land of Many Hands: Women in the American West.* New York: Oxford University Press, 1997.

Spinner, Stephanie. *Little Sure Shot: The Story of Annie Oakley.* New York: Random House, 1993.

Wadsworth, Ginger. *Laura Ingalls Wilder: Storyteller of the Prairie.* Minneapolis: Lerner Publications Company, 1997.

Women's History
http://www.womenshistory.about.com
This site has articles on many aspects of life on the American frontier.

PHOTO ACKNOWLEDGMENTS

The images in this book are used with permission of: Library of Congress, pp. 4, 11, 15 (LC-USZ62-92263), 66, 77, 84; Cahokia Mounds State Historical Site, p. 6; Laura Westlund, pp. 8, 23; Denver Public Library, Western History Collection, pp. 10 (X-33784), 54 (NS-455), 60 (X-21684), 69 (Z-109), 91, 97 (X-21702); Nevada Historical Society, p. 12; © Hulton Archive/Getty Images, p. 14 © Bettmann/CORBIS, pp. 16, 100; Painting by Robert Lindneux, Woolaroc Museum, Bartlesville, OK, p. 18; © The Church of Jesus Christ of Latter-Day Saints, Courtesy of Historical Department. Used by permission, p. 20; Kansas State Historical Society, pp. 22, 73; Wyoming State Archives, Department of State Parks and Cultural Resources, pp. 25, 101; California Department of Parks and Recreation Photographic Archives, p. 27; Courtesy of the Bancroft Library, University of California, Berkeley, p. 30; Fred Hulstrand History in Pictures collection, NDIRS-NDSU, Fargo, p. 33; Laura Ingalls Wilder Memorial Society, De Smet, SD, pp. 35, 40; Nebraska State Historical Society Photograph Collections, p. 36; Laura Ingalls Wilder Home Association, Mansfield, MO, p. 42; Ohio Historical Society, p. 44; Courtesy of Karen Allen, p. 47; Garst Museum, Greenville, Ohio, p. 51; Denver Public Library, Western History Collection, D.F. Barry, B-608, p. 53; Circus World Museum, Baraboo, Wisconsin (BBWW-NL200-98-1U-1), p. 57; Denver Public Library, Western History Collection, Ralph D. Lee, X-61223, p. 63; Denver Public Library, Western History Collection, Cooley Studio, X-21699, p. 64; Denver Public Library, Western History Collection, O.T. Davis, Z-338, p. 71; © Pictorial Parade/Getty Images, p. 79; Adams Memorial Museum, Deadwood, SD; p. 80; Courtesy Arizona Historical Society, Tucson, p. 85; Division of Manuscripts, University of Oklahoma Library, Rose Collection, #2127, p. 88; © R.Y. Young/Hulton Archive/Getty Images, p. 94.
Cover images: Denver Public Library, Western History Collection, D.F. Barry, B-941A (top center), Western History Collection, University of Oklahoma Library (top left), Denver Public Library, Western History Collection, X-21702 (center bottom), Kansas State Historical Society, Topeka (bottom right), Courtesy Arizona Historical Society, Tucson (top right)